The Mind & Heart

George & Lucia

INTRODUCTION

I was born on February 24th, 1954 in Zadar, Croatia and grew up in a small village called Policnik. At the age of 16 my whole family emigrated to Montreal, Canada.

While I was growing up I can truthfully say that I had a joyful childhood. Like most Balkan nations, Croatia is a country that has gone through many wars and whose people have suffered tremendous hardships, but this was transparent to me. In fact, growing up, the material world was the last thing on my mind. I was extremely sensitive to people and 'feelings' and this was the world I perceived and was born into.

Deep questions and emotions took center stage and throughout my childhood the spiritual and impossible-to-answer questions of old often plagued me: Why do people argue and fight? Why do men abuse women and why do parents and teachers whip their kids? Why do we have to go to school on Christmas? Why is there poverty, and why are there wars? Why does God punish us? Unlike the other kids around me, the fact that I could not answer these questions left me with internal anguish.

I was a very sensitive child. It would take very little for me to be overwhelmed with emotion and occasionally I would faint. In fact, if I got screamed at by an adult, or if there was even the slightest suggestion of physical harm, I'd pass out.

The adults around me very quickly learned not to expose me to either of these, and this in turn made correcting my bad behaviors a significant challenge for them.

I was disobedient and protested on many issues regarding my upbringing, and my blackouts kept most adult reprimanding at bay. It is possible that due to my relative 'safety' from adult authority figures I had a deep fear of God's authoritative powers. Like most Croatians, I was raised Christian, went to church every Sunday, and was a faithful believer. However, I wasn't able to establish a bond of love with God because I thought He was far away and would only make an appearance if I sinned. Even though throughout most of my adult life I held the belief that God was somewhere far away and impossible to reach, I never ceased to pray and always hoped to get closer to Him wherever He was.

As I got older, I devoted myself to prayer and meditation. I also read many books on spiritual growth and I gained quite a bit of knowledge, although it always seemed that I was far from understanding the point of my existence and my sensibilities. I kept questioning absolutely everything but I could not figure out the true meaning of my life and my sensitivity often made me unhappy. It wasn't that my life was really that bad, but it was more of a feeling that I felt something was missing and I wanted to find out what. I prayed to Christ to give me strength and wisdom to see my path clearly, to know my purpose and to know and serve God. I had done everything that was possible to attain inner peace, yet I was consumed with struggles between meaning and reason. The malcontent and questioning remained in my mind and I prayed and asked our Saviour Jesus Christ for a response...

...And I got an answer! The answer was actually a simple yet profound question: 'who am I?' Answering this question was very hard, even scary to me, so before trying to do so, I searched the phrase online…'who am I?'

As is often the case when researching this kind of thing on the internet, I was redirected and bounced around too many websites to track. Each new link clearly described the power behind the question and pushed me forward. Through this experience and a very significant discovery of the spiritual master Mooji's teachings, a whole new field of personal observation was revealed. I started discovering a great deal about my identity, my perceptions, my conditions and limitations, as well as where they came from.

Ego was a word that I was constantly confronted with and I came to understand that my ego was the main obstacle for all my hardships.

Armed with this new understanding of ego, and through prolonged meditation, as well as taking in the words of wisdom from my research, I started shedding so many wrong concepts, thoughts, beliefs and ideas of who I was and who I thought I was when growing up. Life with my parents in the village came back in a new clarity and perspective and it all had a cascade effect culminating in a new horizon of my reality opening up before me. This was my spiritual awakening! It was deep and wide and was brought into my consciousness in jarring clarity.

This awakening experience had a physical effect as well; for days I was unable to move. It was like the child in me had fainted, but I was still awake. I was frozen still and unable to fill even basic needs like feeding myself. My sensitive spirit was overwhelmed and I had to find a way to channel my findings. I started to write, and after hours of trance-like typing, a conversation between my mind and heart, emerged.

PROLOGUE

Let me take you on a fascinating trip to meet two mysterious energy forces that in tandem continually commune and struggle; my mind and heart- George and Lucia. They share the same space, and work at each other's side each and every day. They are, by God's command, purposefully sent to experience their two entirely different and often contradictory worlds of existence, together.

They go about their daily routine, each doing their best to live in accordance with the laws of both Heaven and Earth. As they are unaware of their most essential purpose, however, they continually experience misunderstanding and conflict which hinder their stride forward on the path of life.

Lucia is wise to their journey towards freedom and happiness, but her attempts to persuade George to follow her soft footsteps are regularly thwarted. George is blurred to Lucia's chosen path, clinging rather to the conviction that his is the best and only way. And in the face of that defiance, Lucia is stifled and finds no peace.

In the fullness of time, Lucia learns to soothe her suffering by making sense of what George wants and she appeals to him; that lack of awareness is indeed the only problem they have.

Inspired by love and understanding, Lucia takes George on a nostalgic trip, so that together, they may learn from their memories. George, just the same, remembers often the bad times and forgets the good.

George is largely distracted or altogether absent. Clearly, this makes conversation a difficult task. Lucia, in patience, nonetheless endeavors to speak of her puzzlement about his choices. Not unusual is it that George has trouble understanding what exactly Lucia means and because of that he grows so stressed and enraged that he chooses to flee without a trace, leaving Lucia behind in the grips of great despair.

By great fortune, Lucia can calm the iron determination of George, and gently show him that the main source of their suffering is the delusion of his ego's false identity! Once he awakens and realizes who he truly is, their purpose will become what they were always meant to be, a true union of the mind and heart in serenity, joy and peace.

THE CONVERSATION

One rare evening, when opportunity arose, Lucia managed to hold George's attention:

"I am sure you are finding me tiresome, but I can no longer hold it in.

I really find it hard to understand why you are always absent, roaming the outside world.

Please do not get me wrong. Out there is indeed interesting, precisely because it has infinite charms and beauty that we can never fully absorb even if we lived hundreds of lives.

But that is not what concerns me; it is your endless excursions out, which clearly draws you away from spending time at home, for I am eager that we be together. It seems you are no longer interested.

I do not hear your warm words or feel your desire to even look at me.

You are not looking forward to my presence.

You are not looking forward to my carefully prepared meals.

You do not enjoy my tireless hard work to keep our home neat and comfortable.

You hardly ever notice my beauty that I devote to you.

A vase of fresh flowers on our table does not draw your attention.

You do not admire our candle flame, a symbol of our deep love.

What is going on my beloved?

What is causing you to be so cold and distant?

I miss you."

George abruptly gets up, and restlessly paces back and forth. He cannot restrain himself and shouts angrily:

"There you go again with that same old story. What do you want from me?

I'm extremely resourceful! A decent life doesn't come without difficulty and effort, you know?!

I toil and my work is not easy. It takes much out of me. You just don't realize!

I carry an enormous burden on my shoulders.

You are clueless to how I stay afloat."

"There are times, for sure, I want nothing more than to escape.

But that would be cowardly--and I'm no coward; never was, never will be.

I learned to fight and overcome.

Many scorn weakness and cowardice-

I refuse to go to such depths and be seen that way."

"And I've heard you say that even the most poor

folk are not cowards.

That they are not afraid of hard work or of death!

As much as I admire their strength and resilience,

I wish to also possess wealth.

So please let me work so that we can prosper."

In remarkable contrast to George's loud and

righteous tone, Lucia responds softly and

sensitively,

"I hear you, my beloved.

I know the virtue of your work.

It is a necessity that I truly appreciate.

But often, I feel, you are doing too much,

You are over-stretched.

You cannot even find peace in your sleep;

I see you in bed twitch like a fish on a hook.

And no matter what remedies you take, they obviously do not help!"

"I ask with genuine love and respect;

Do you dwell and overexert in thought?

Maybe we can look at other ways to find you rest?

May I share with you the refuge that is our inner world?

The prayers, the invocation to God- in which you can find freedom?

The silence and peace that no amount of money could buy?"

George, as usual, is agitated. He looks away and acts as if he is not listening.

With a good-natured smile, Lucia continues:

"We have never sat in silence together and prayed like we used to when we were kids.

We have never meditated together.

As much as a prayer is powerful, the sound of silence is equally compelling.

It can be a piercing scream to the Heavens.

Bear with me, my beloved. I have practiced this my entire life.

There is much wisdom inside. It is deeply rewarding.

It would be a wonderful way to be together and alone, to feel each other's presence, the presence of existence, the presence of God.

I am convinced you will not regret it."

These words were too much for George, no matter how valuable or farfetched. For it is difficult to pay heed to the suggestion of one we do not respect.

And George's estimation of Lucia as weak and naive certainly is no exception.

"You obviously don't get it! You never get it!

Stop shaking that head of yours and start to think for a change!

Enough about feelings. Where exactly have they taken you, tell me, I pray?

You are deep in delusion, I'll tell you that! Wake from your slumber and look at reality in the eye.

There is no time for fantasy. We have to roll up our sleeves and pull our own weight."

"You've no idea what it means to be in the real world.

Why not take a good look and see what the outside is really like?

You'll behold the immense riches people posses and unyielding pleasures they enjoy.

And how do you think they come about their exquisite meals and their finest wines?

By feelings, you say? No! By the power of thoughts and actions, my dear.

We've been endowed with our intellect to succeed in life.

We've been fashioned with our will to get what we want.

Think, why don't you?! All these prayers, meditation and whatsoever you are talking about will choke our success."

Skillful in this commotion, and yet, sensitive to their interminable differences, Lucia tenderly speaks from a position of kinship and understanding; she is familiar with the wide deception of thought,

"We, my beloved, are two ends of a rope stretched over a fire pit.

Like thought and feeling, we tug back and forth at the same time.

Beautifully, gloriously in harmony.

As a restful flower and its alluring fragrance.

You and I, my precious love, are of the same essence.

One without the other cannot be.

We would otherwise tumble both into the fire."

Lucia carries on,

"There are many books, with many words, offering much knowledge.

But it is light that enables us to read.

And that manifests our reflection."

George only addresses her last point,

"Are you saying that I don't know who I am?

Don't be so naive. I know full well who I am and what I'm capable of.

Do YOU know who you are?!

All you know is to say- "help this one and help that one", or,

"love him, love her, give here, give there, be understanding, be compassionate."

Who are YOU in all this?

And who is helping you?

Who is supporting you?

I'll tell you -- I'm the one, the only one who always stands by you.

Tirelessly protecting and supporting you

You somehow have the gall to tell me,

I don't know who I am, and I make no time for

you.

For us to be together, you need to respect me.

This is certainly not the case and you need to

change your ways."

In unbounded goodness, Lucia paused and then

started again in a warm affirmation,

"My nature is made of love and I cannot be

anything else.

You are also love, my beloved, only you forgot.

The love in your being matches my own.

You have to turn inward to see it, to feel it.

You used to be loving and creative.

Remember how many poems we wrote back then?

We thought that the whole nature was of poetic origin and the most beautiful instrumental composition.

We longed for the wild, and felt the endless vibrations that travelled through the air-

As if the sun, the moon and the stars were swinging in the endless sky, orchestrating thousand celestial symphonies.

We thought that every sound was moving toward us and we were the center of it all-

A feeling that gave us a profound silence, peace and joy.

And we celebrated because nature was a sheer celebration, a womb of thousand creative images."

"But to be creative, we need to fall in love with existence.

Without love, life has no meaning, has no colors; without love, churches and temples would be ordinary dwellings.

We have to create the meaning within our being and within our innermost core of existence through our prayers.

Our prayers will cleanse our thoughts and throw out all the rubbish that we have been carrying for so many years.

Our prayers can remove the ignorance from our eyes, like the rising sun dispels the darkness of the night.

Our prayers should be a true expression of love for God and His resurrected Son, Jesus Christ, who lived for us, who died for us.

Remember the village feast on the day of Christ's resurrection, one of the greatest Christian impulses, one of the most celebrated day of the year?

Every rural resident went to church on that day to be part of the Holy Mass, where they all gained new impetus, new energy, and the newly restored faith-

That gave them all the firmer hope for a better and stronger tomorrow."

"We also must renew our love for God and for each other, my beloved.

We must be unconditional in loving and to not ask anything in return; love for the sheer joy of love."

Now George responds,

"Please don't talk to me about love and poetry.

Talk to me about something realistic.

There is no such thing as love.

Do you actually believe that the world cares for love?

I don't think people come together for the sake of love!

So please talk to me about money, the currency that the whole world loves and respects.

Why is it that you never bring up the subject of that reality?

Is it because you have no interest in it, or you have no need for it?

I guess you don't, you have plenty of money!

Because I'm the one who takes care of it and brings it home.

You only know how to spend my money.

You only know how to give to others, whether they deserve it or not."

Lucia replies,

"It is not about deserving, it is about giving, without any conditions, without any expectations.

This may be giving of anything.

We can give joy to others and make them feel joyous.

We can share our compassion with others so they too feel compassionate.

The more we share our love, our blessings, our happiness with others, the more we will learn that life has become generous to us in many ways.

Jesus said: "Love your neighbors as you love yourself."

This is not just a common teaching of day-to-day morality; this is a fundamental and significant truth.

But, to love our neighbor as we love ourselves, we first need to love God.

When we love God, we do not have problem loving our neighbor or the whole existence.

To love God it means to be in love with our consciousness.

With our consciousness we can love trees, animals, birds, mountains, oceans, suns, moons, and stars.

When we love consciously, our inner being sprouts, our intelligence multiplies, our knowledge expands.

When we give freely, without expecting anything in return, our giving becomes a tremendous inner joy.

By giving we do not lose anything, we only gain more.

We receive what we give. In fact we always receive more than we give."

George continues to argue,

"You remind me of our father, he was just like you.

He did not know how to take care of his things.

Whoever needed something he was the first one to offer.

Our mother always told him not to be so generous.

But the poor man had never listened to her.

What exactly did he receive back?

Nothing!

He was a great thinker but he had no chance to act upon it.

He did not have possibility or the opportunity."

George carries on,

"Rural conditions were poor and unsatisfactory.

Do you remember, that we did not have water in the house?

And because we did not have water, we also had no toilet.

We had to go to the woods to relieve ourselves.

And when we finished there was no paper to wipe ourselves, we used whatever was at hand-

Whether grass, oak leaves or pebbles,

and so, we always left a mark on our underwear for our mother to wash.

I hope you remember that!"

"Do you remember how many times she would go to the village well back and forth, to get us water on her poor head?

The large quantity she had to bring to wash our dirty underwear and the rest of the laundry every single week, everything by hand...

It would take her an entire morning of endless scrubbing and washing.

I hope you remember all that."

Lucia responds,

"Of course I do my beloved, how could I forget!

Just a thought of it causes me great sadness.

I can only imagine how difficult it was for mother to carry those buckets of water on her head.

It was just like everyone else in the village, where only the women were responsible for that need.

Yet, we never heard them complain, they were happy that they had the well to be able to get to the water.

We never saw any rural men ever going to the well to fetch water because of their great pride.

They were ashamed to carry water through the village.

Did you ever see our father going to the well?"

George responds,

"I didn't but, he was the first one in the village who eventually changed the water situation and I'm proud of him.

Do you remember how long it took him to actually succeed?

It took him one whole summer to dig a deep pit in the ground and establish a water tank for rainwater to flow in.

It wasn't an easy job to do since he had no special tools. First, he had to lay mines to break the stones, and later, take it all out by his hands and a shovel.

It was a huge ordeal!"

Lucia responds,

"Yes, I remember the rural neighbors coming to inspect what he was up to, but that no one actually helped him with anything.

It was in the village order, to help each other at every opportunity.

However, in this situation they did not bother at all, since they did not believe in his project.

A few of them mocked our father, asking him to let them know when he tastes the water from his alleged water tank."

George says,

"He eventually managed to bring his project into existence and with that, liberated our mother from carrying heavy buckets of water back and forth from the well.

His project set an example in the village and everyone eventually did the same thing."

Lucia responds,

"It was always harder for the women.

They never had any time for themselves.

Each of them worked hard to serve and obey; their sense of contribution was their religion.

They served God, church, and their family, honorably and loyally.

Nothing seemed impossible to bear and even if it was, no one would know, since they never took time to complain.

They were always busy, forever running and working, and often we could hear them singing as a sign of their lightness and humility.

They were up long before sunrise; kneading the dough every single morning, baking, cooking, ironing, knitting, sewing, laboring in the fields.

They did absolutely everything."

"These women were bold, brave and beautiful. They never worried about aging, nor ever spoke of menopause.

Nobody could hear them talk about suffering hot flashes, headaches, dizziness or whatsoever of any physical discomfort.

They did not do anything to hold on to their youth or never cried about it passing.

Getting old was a natural life process and they gladly accepted it.

In fact, they were happy to be liberated from all their environmental responsibilities so they could finally rest."

FURTHER OBSERVATION

Now George takes over,

"Can you imagine that most of those women used to give birth at home?

They refused to visit the gynecologist while pregnant.

They were terribly shy.

The social care did not agree with this behavior and soon, required physicians to regularly visit the pregnant women in every village.

But, that too was a problem.

In our village, when the women found out that the gynecologist was coming to the village, they would scatter and flee into the woods where they hid until the doctor left the village."

Lucia responds to this,

"They did not care for they were certain that nothing would happen to them or their babies.

According to their village rule, they would, "eat a healthy diet, pray to God, and find the best midwife in the area".

As much as healthy food and prayers were important to them, it was also crucial that the midwife have a good and humble spirit.

Since the midwife was to be the first who received the baby in her arms, she had to be of warm nature, so the infant would feel a kind and friendly welcome into this world."

Lucia carries on,

"Do you remember that cold winter day, when we walked to neighbors house and witnessed a midwife as she prepared a woman for birth.

First, she lit a candle, and then brought several loads of straw, and placed it next to the hearth full of fire.

The candle, as a sign of light and prayer; the straw, to serve as a bed for the woman; and the fire, to keep both the mother and her baby warm.

Then, the mother-to-be and the midwife kneeled down to pray, calling the mother of God for protection through the entire labor process.

I also recall that the older women thought that hospitals were cold and unappealing compared to their home.

They said, "there are no candles at the hospital and also no prayers, no straw, no fire, and often, not even a nurse!

Of course, back then, the maternity nurses were cold and rude..."

George promptly interrupts to speak of healthcare services:

"At any hospital, both the doctors and the nurses were accepting bribes from their patients.

The more bribe, the better the service.

Although, bribes have been abolished since Croatia became independent.

For a long time, I thought that our country was the only one where bribes for doctors and nurses were allowed.

But then I realized that it also exists in the rich western countries as well: the only difference being that in the village the bribe was with food whereas there, it's done with money.

I remember the villagers gave their most valuable foods to the doctors like, dried ham, chicken, turkey, and lamb.

The food that they themselves could not enjoy every day, but saved for special occasions like holidays, baptism, confirmations and weddings.

And if a sick man didn't have enough valuable food items to offer to the hospital staff, he would have to wait long in line, to get his turn to get examined.

Apparently, even the cleaning ladies would demand gifts if a patient wanted to have his or her room cleaned!"

George initiates the topic of electricity, and laments,

"We also had no electricity!

Do you remember how difficult it was to find the way in the dark?

Whether in the house or outside!

A candlelight was the only means of illumination-

What a life we had!"

Lucia responds,

"Come on my beloved, it was not that bad.

The villagers had no idea what it meant to have electricity and hence functioned, as they would have with it.

Everything was done properly and on time.

Each rural house had countless candles that the women with their skillful hands had made and shaped, illuminating every room of their homes. While the country hearth served their various household needs."

"On the hearth, they cooked and baked. Next to it they recited their holy prayers, enjoyed their meals and toasted their homemade wine.

Do you remember the Christmas holidays, when the country hearth was constantly burning with an overwhelming fire? Especially on Christmas Eve, as a sign of tireless anticipation of Christ's glorious birth.

This was when it was tradition to search through forests in pursuit of large oak logs, often three, in the sign of the Trinity.
The logs were brought home, cleaned, dried and prepared for a ritual. The whole family would gather."

"Commonly, the oldest male in the family would sprinkle the log with holy water, olive oil, wine, wheat grains, reciting a prayer.
The log was placed on the hearth on Christmas Eve, and left to burn in flames for as long as it could.
When the log completely burned, women would collect the ashes and sprinkle them on their every

field, as a sign of abundant fruits in the coming season.

And they never forgot to sprinkle some in the field of their neighbors as a signal of affection and respect for one another.

The rural hearth was truly a symbol of home, where the fire was burning every single day."

Lucia then recalls the Gypsies who used to pass by their village,

"As they came to the village, the colorful gypsies pitched their tents in the nearby woods.

Immediately upon their settlement, each village woman would pick up their broken pots and pans and carry them off to gypsy tents and leave them there to be fixed.

While the gypsy men repaired our utensils, their wives went from door to door reading the destiny of every village woman.

Yes, they were always moving around, never lingering long, as if they were always in a hurry.

They travelled in their caravans and defied the sun, the rain and the rough storms.

Never caring about the importance of time, never thinking of tomorrow.

They journeyed aimlessly, without a plan or even a faith.

Away from all liabilities, away from all laws, wandering from one end of the globe to another.

Playing their old violins and singing their saddest songs; waking up every notion of human life longing."

WORLD OUTLOOK

Lucia returns to subject of electricity,

"Electricity came to the village a few years later and with that arrived so much more responsibility.

They all had to buy electrical appliances and television sets and it was a big deal because they were poor.

They had to work much harder to buy it all.

Prior to that they did not think as much.

They were more at peace.

Eventually all of them bought appliances and television sets, and by that time it seemed that much had changed in those people.

Their ego awakened and took them to another stage of being, forcing them to compete among each other.

Most of them wanted to buy something more expensive and better than what their neighbors had.

Younger people were glued to their television set, staring at the screen with great curiosity about life and the world.

TV was the ultimate door into someone else's kitchen or bedroom.

Watching how other people lived inspired them to seek similar experiences.

Young people came to be crazy for modern footwear and clothing.

Many of them took the bus to neighboring Italy to buy something unique and fashionable. Once back home, they would show off their purchases to the others.

Soon after they started talking of escaping from the village in pursuit of a better life.

Seeing what others had caused them suffering.

They started to hate the countryside and everything about it."

George starts,

"Do you blame them?

Anyone would have ran away from there if they had anywhere else to escape. But they did not have the chance and lived completely bound to their miseries."

 Lucia responds,

"I'm sorry but they were unaware that they actually had a good life.

Their environment was fresh, quiet and peaceful.

All of the country food was chemical-free.

People never fed their crops or their livestock with anything artificial.

The air was clean and transparent such that one could hear someone talk from a mile away.

Do you remember when we listened to the howling of wolves in the night, when it seemed to us as if they were at our door?

Everything was so pure, peaceful and pleasant.

After all, isn't it that the village was indeed the place where in reality all became? In the village the first love was born, the first song sung, and initial poetry written.

Famous giants and kings have sprung up in rural lap.

The first revolt was raised in the village and first blood was shed.

So was God born in a village barn…"

"Rural life has always been far easier, cleaner, quieter and more interesting than any city.

How many people nowadays are fleeing from city to village to shelter themselves from the screeching and threatening noise so they can find a favorable peace.

Only in the village can one be calm and rested.

And it was only when electricity came to the village that people started changing. It seemed as if they lost part of their peace because they had to get all the electrical supplies, which gave them quite a bit of stress that they previously did not have.

Television caused them to communicate less and spend less time with each other.

And on account of all that, old people said:

"To hell with electricity and whoever first invented it!"

They were unaware that it was their neighbor Tesla who actually electrified the world."

George responds,

"Tesla was indeed one of the world's greatest geniuses.

He created fortune for multitude of people but he himself died penniless since his many works were stolen.

Why good people always end badly?

Why so many honorable people through the whole human history ended up on the cross of pain and suffering?

Justice is cruel!

Let us take a good look at Alojzije Stepinac who, after his hundreds of good deeds was thrown into prison and brutally tortured!

When in reality he saved and protected countless people during the bloody war!

He saved Catholics, Jews, Orthodox, Muslims, Gypsies!

He did not choose people by religion or profession!

He saved all of them to end up paying for it with a martyr's death!

Or take a good look at Martin Luther who fought so hard to protect human integrity and human rights!

To liberate the innocent from the iron-hard jaws of injustice!

That he would eventually get executed without a grain of remorse…!

I could go on but who will hear me?

The criminals of this world will continue to exert their bloody deeds!

To later die and be called as good people!"

George continues,

"You should actually learn something from all this!

And start looking at the world from a different angle because people are not as they appear to be.

I'm telling you, do not be so good and generous!

Be bad, be corrupt!

Because bad people always end up well in life.

They know that after they die they will be called as good people regardless of who they were and what they did.

Do not trust people!

People do not care who you are and how you feel.

They just want to take advantage of you.

Most people are careless and selfish.

They will step on anyone to reach their desired goal and never think of their bad karma, if it even exists!

They have no fear of any punishment.

It is not 'as you sow, so shall you reap.'

Many people do bad and never pay for their actions.

There is no justice for it can't be!

It's not enough to talk about certain individuals only, you need to look at the whole picture of the world.

Or maybe just look at Croatian people and their destiny.

They have, for centuries, been plundered and persecuted although they have never stolen and snatched anything from anyone.

Never did they forcefully take a thing, simply because the majority are good and honest.

And when a man is good he is also naive.

Their naivety had led them to find themselves in many wars throughout history; where they shed rivers of blood, always innocent.

How can anyone feel sorry for those people?

They are themselves the cause of their sufferings.

The world is not measured by goodness; it requires an intensive use of thinking.

The value of goodness is only among people who never want any gain in life, who are satisfied with nothing.

Not to mention our parent's generation in the distant past.

They were mere paupers!

They had no food!

Their barns were empty!

The war caused poisoning, which destroyed every seed planted in the ground, and nothing could sprout and grow.

They were hungry, barefoot and naked!

They had no food and no medicine!

Alas, countless children died because of scarcity of medicines!"

George is still on subject of poverty,

"You don't know what it means to be poor!

They were all desperate!

Did you forget when they used to say,

"Almighty God, when are you going to send us something better because, what we have is not worthy of anything."

At other times, they used to praise the poor,

with a conviction, that the poor man was more likely to reach Heaven than the rich?

God, where did they get such a belief?

Or were they saying this to convince themselves of this illusory truth as a prevention from going insane!"

"Regardless of what they said and what they lived through, I know only one thing and that is, I would not ever wish to live such life!

Because, it was not worth living!

And furthermore, what did our parents have?

They had nothing!

Neither savings nor cars; they had no jewelry, they never traveled, and they never enjoyed anything.

Not to mention how they lived their youth!

Our father said that as a teenager he would work in the fields all day long and when he'd come home, there was no dinner.

He would go to bed hungry!

Can you imagine that?

Our father had no freedom to create or build a thing!

His hands and his intellect were restrained!

He was crushed by the burden of his family!

Because whatever he wanted to start, the family was against it!

What kind of life did he really have?"

"Everyone lived in difficult family circles back then.

Every village house was full of people.

They had no space to breathe and had no freedom to speak.

There were often more than two brothers in the house, all married with children.

None of them were allowed to build their own nest and move out.

These people suffocated and suffered but never expressed their opinion.

It was a shame to move out.

A father could not imagine any of his sons to leave the house.

They listened and obeyed to whatever he had to say.

Father indeed was a God and a bludgeon-

What kind of life was that?"

"And what did we have as kids?

Have you forgotten that we slept on a wide bag filled with dry corn leaves?!"

Lucia responds,

"I have not forgotten, and I was glad to feel the breath of nature under our body. In fact that did not last long. Our mother shortly after made us a comfortable mattress from sheep wool."

George begins again,

"Our life was modest!

We were given the bare basics.

We hardly had anything to wear-a piece of clothing for school and church, and one for around the house.

We never received a gift for birthday or for Christmas.

The only gifts that we ever received were the fruits of our parent's labor in the fields.

I refuse to remember such a life!"

Lucia felt it important to mention the many good and valuable qualities that the village people actually had. George does not speak fairly.

"Those people, despite their modest and often hard living conditions, had great honor and respect for one another. Far more than people have today, be it in the village or in the city.

They believed in the power of holy orders and thought highly of them.

They went to church every Sunday and they were good role models to their children. They always brought up their ancient proverbs and their values to remind their offspring to stay on the right path.

They taught their children to be good and exemplary. To be diligent, and to work hard like ants in the field, like bees in the hive.

They taught them to preserve and cherish their assets as a holy oil and, to always share with others. To never live in greed of any kind. To never steal from others because anything stolen would be cursed by God.

And to always praise the power of heavenly Father because, without Him they will never have peace and joy."

Lucia approaches George with a little disappointment because of his expressions of dishonesty and belittling.

"George, Please, let this be the last of your insults addressed to our past.

Please do not embarrass our deceased, and do not under validate their integrity.

Do not step on their hard labor.

You have no right to look down on them.

Please, silence your arrogance and curb your pride.

How can you allow your ego to rule your life?

You can not keep decorating your ego.

It is not a decoration but a form of suicide.

You are destroying yourself.

Your ego surrounds your intelligence like a thick layer of darkness.

Your bondage to your rotten thoughts is your suffering.

It is your slavery.

There is no greater sin or punishment than ignorance.

Your ego is darkness.

Your intelligence is light.

Your intelligence needs to grow, expand, and flow.

It needs a vast space like the sky, to move towards life's creativity.

In your deep conditioning only your ego can survive.

Not your intelligence.

Through the power of your ego, you could fall down and kiss the dust and you could, by God's justice, never again ascend to your royal seat."

Lucia continues,

"Pull yourself together and see that our parents gave us all that a child really needs.

They gave us everything they could and cared for us in their best way.

Please do not cut the parts that are precious and valuable.

Do not insult the power of soil on which they shed their sweat.

So that they could give us all of those gifts without which you and I could not have survived.

Please start remembering how much you used to love the fields, the meadows and the forest.

And the whole rich gifts which Nature gave us.

How much you admired her space and beauty.

How can you not be aware?

How can you not have appreciation?

You must know that Nature is a Goddess of all that exists.

She is providing the air for every breath we take.

Her power runs through our veins nourishing our blood.

She does not give merely by selection, nor does she have a sense of prejudice.

She never once provided less to the one and more to the other.

Never kept the score of who deserves more.

She willingly gives for the sake of existence.

Without her honorable gifts both you and I would simply perish."

George did not see this coming and he does not see this conversation as very helpful. On the contrary, his ego is highly offended and it prompts him to leave.

GEORGE LEAVES

George runs away and does not return for many days and nights, without leaving any sign for Lucia to trace or find him.

Lucia grew so scared thinking that he may never come back that she wrote him a letter full of sadness in which she brought back memories that they experienced together in their childhood:

"If you knew how much I miss you, my beloved.

If you knew how I feel since you disappeared.

If you knew the pain in my being-

I always feel you, my love, wondering where you are.

And what you're doing in your distant world.

I cannot sleep in peace at night.

My thoughts often haunt me.

They sometimes lead me to think of the worst.

God forbid you're not well, as it would make me break.

But I pray to heavenly Grace to care for you and to protect you.

For you to stand alive and well.

So you come back home to me as soon as possible.

I'm desperately waiting for you, my beloved, like you and I have been waiting for swallows to return every spring from the far South.

Yesterday I was in church to light a candle and pray deeply in the name of your imminent return to me.

Remember how many times we went to church?

To kneel and humbly pray to Christ for all our living and deceased souls, hoping to be blessed with at least a trickle of His sacred power."

Lucia continues,

"If you knew how much you mean to me.

I miss you!

I miss you like a cold February misses the warm sun.

Like a thirsty field misses the rain in summer drought.

I miss you as a young girl misses her lover.

Like an orphan misses a warm embrace of a mother.

I always need you close to me, my beloved.

Your presence makes me happy and satisfied.

With you, I become so much more alive.

Like in those days of our childhood, when we used to play together.

Ah, my love!

Those precious moments can not be forgotten.

They are deeply rooted in my being.

The memory of us running through the fields,
wandering around the meadows in Spring.

When the nature was at its best.

When everything was green and exuberant.

Where we ran happy and carefree, chasing
gorgeous butterflies

to gently catch them and then to let them go.

We kept admiring bees harvesting pollen.

How they created the honey and sweetened the
whole village!

We picked a variety of alluring flowers.

Some we kept for us, some we brought to our
mother.

Forever tirelessly fleeing, always barefoot and
bare-chest.

As far as our eyes could see, as far as our thoughts could stretch.

Always in flight of curiosity.

Our wings have never been silent-"

GEORGE'S RETURN

One fine day, George came back home seemingly calm and composed. But, one can tell that he is still offended and insulted. And he needs to express it to Lucia. He wants to tell her once and for all how he really feels.

George begins,

"While I was away, I had a long time to think and analyze our situation.

I came to the conclusion that, you and I can not live together.

We have absolutely nothing in common.

Even though I knew it before and suffered all this time thinking you'd change.

But I see that it is hardly possible and therefore, either I move out or you do.

I cannot take it any more.

The more I wait, the more I waste my time.

And, time is all I really have.

I no longer wish to dissipate it talking with you about the past.

I have a future to think of and, anticipate what needs are to arrive.

The future is all I'm interested in, but it cannot be with you.

I cannot let you constrain my plans for a better and richer life.

You forever entangle me so that I can not move forward."

Lucia is speechless. She can not believe what George just said. George obviously does not see anything wrong with himself.

Now George continues with the rest of his intention,

"You never once got curious about my business.

Never peered to see how everything is going.

Never contributed to anything.

You've never provided anything to this dwelling.

Never showed any interest in my accomplishments.

Never cared how much money comes in or goes out.

You have no sense of respect for my invested efforts.

I'm tired of you not recognizing me.

I'm fed up of you constantly judging me."

LUCIA LEAVES

Lucia was profoundly hurt and deeply humiliated by George but did not say a word. She left him enough time to swallow his words and think it over. Meanwhile, she left the house and went to the lake to gather herself from the emotional shock. Here, she will write yet another letter to George, which will possibly be the last.

It was difficult for Lucia to start writing anything at all. Her tears were trickling down and her sobs were choking her. She wanted to die right there and then.

It was overwhelming. It was the first time that George ever acted this way. It was unbelievably hard for her to understand why he was so saddened and why he wanted to separate.

He must be literally losing all his reasoning. Lucia is nothing but goodness and love.

Eventually, Lucia gathered some strength and managed to finish her letter.

In which she wrote,

"If you hurt me so deeply, I know I will cry.

I will cry for the sake of my living soul.

I will cry for the sake of my integrity.

I will cry for the sake of my profound love for you.

I will shed my tears because you are rejecting me.

And never allowing me to get close and be one with you.

That hurts deeply.

I will cry when the winds are madly blowing across the garments of grey-dry autumn,

when snowstorms take a stand in cold winter.

I will cry when the colorful spring arrives,

When the sun shines in a hot summer season.

I will shed my tears for the sake of our destiny for we are made for each other.

I will cry for us to remain together.

For us to be as one.

To honor and worship God in heaven.

To learn and grow into maturity of knowing.

To break-open our illusory world for the sake of our awakening.

I will weep so loud that you will hear me.

But if you remain deaf, unwilling to change,

Great sadness will arise within my being.

I will deeply desire to disappear.

I will let the abyss swallow me.

And when I get out of this chaos,

When my consciousness starts clearing up,

I will weep even more.

I will shout ever so loud and call God in heaven,

to spill down on my chest, a handful of celestial powder

so I can forgive you for everything-

And when my being is silent and calm.

When my tears are dry.

I will still cry-

But when a new dawn swiftly appears,

When the sunrise kisses the sky,

And all the storms of sadness pass away,

When the river of tears reach the ocean,

And all my wounds get thoroughly healed.

When you start to remember-

When your thoughts become restless

Disturbing your peace, driving you mad,

When you cannot sleep during the night,

You cannot function during the day,

When your notion starts to cut your psyche,

When you become sad and powerless like that bird
whose nest the village kids destroyed and whose
delightful offspring they threw away.

And when the desire emerges within your being
because you miss me and you want me back
I won't be there any longer -
Because in me, a deep desire has awakened to
disappear from it all."

Lucia pauses and starts again,

"When I come back to my own dwelling, near and
far of the same coast,
Where warm rays of brilliant sun start kissing my
hair, my face, my lips
I will fly high.

I will soar the skies with the mountain eagle and touch her untouchable nest.

I shall visit a land of wild creatures and dance with the wolf, the stag and the deer.

I will fill up my basket with healing sage and burn it on the hearth fire.

The symbol of our home-

Once again I will light a candle and let it burn through eternity.

Let it melt every illusion.

Let it destroy the chains of slavery-

I shall embrace the pervasive silence of our cradle.

I shall kiss the dust of our ancestors who lived and died and never realized the true meaning of life.

I will again hold our father's hand in gratitude of his deep wisdom.

I will again humbly recite our mother's prayers.

I will pledge my love to them over and over again, for without them I would not be-

I shall wear a fiery torch, my beloved.

I shall kneel down at the altar of our village church and pray Almighty God to give me power.

So I can telepathically burn every trace of your ego.

So you can turn into celestial being.

Then I will take a nice long break in my deep silence and calm.

In the lap of a profound emptiness.

I will let the breeze of the southern wind to gently envelope my being.

I shall breathe the air that tastes like olive oil.

I shall get drunk from the wine of life.

In my deep silence and calm where no thoughts will come forth, when my soul grows firm as a mountain stone and soft as the wool of a lamb,

no words will arrive,

I will have nothing to say."

When Lucia finished writing her last letter to George, she placed it in the mailbox for him to receive it and read it.

The same day she left to go to a silent retreat and stayed there for some time. Here she was able to relax and feel nothing.

These days of total silence was an amazing contribution to Lucia.

Her inner being vibrating with the new and fresh energy of peace. Meanwhile George, as he found himself alone, did not feel that good. As much as he was requesting their separation, when he realized that Lucia was no longer there, he began thinking different thoughts. The thoughts of fear and of unpleasant emotions. He felt that nothing was the same without Lucia in his vicinity.

It all seemed empty and deserted. He even felt abandoned, and forgotten like an orphan and felt sorry for himself. A storm of thoughts continuously echoed in his head, a flood of mixed emotions kept throwing him off balance. He was losing his peace and he could not rest.

But, regardless of his emotional charge and how he felt of being alone at home, or in the world, it was very difficult for George to fully understand, appreciate and love Lucia. He simply could not enter and move through the dimension of unconditional love, compassion and gratitude.

On one hand, he wanted Lucia to respond to him in a loving way, but on the other, if she did, that would frighten him.

He needed her to validate and support him but, too much of that would cause him to panic. It seemed hard for him to find a balance between them and set proper boundaries, so he could trust the ground to show his true nature.

But he did not trust Lucia and he did not believe in any shade of love. He believed that people come together in order to use and take advantage of each other, and that they were not honest with one another.

He claimed that love relationship was a bondage, since there are expectations, demands and, frustrations. He saw that there was a chance from both sides to dominate the other, resulting in a struggle for power.

He claimed that one needs to surrender, usually the weaker one, for the sake of a healthy communion.

Nevertheless, surrendering for the sake of relationship is not a proper approach, surrendering to love is the way to go. George does not grasp that loving warmth is not a poetic event but a reality of significant importance. He cannot see that they could be very loving together without surrendering to one another. Love in their union is indeed a nutriment for their body and soul, when they can perceive, acknowledge and understand through the eyes of the other.

However George needs to drop his ego, which is easier said than done. He has harbored his ego from birth and his ego is not one specific thing. It is made of countless different beliefs that appeared to be true. His convictions became his Self-image, a social mask that thrived on constant approval and control. He wanted to control because he lived in fear. And his greatest fear always was that he would not have enough.

He was defining himself through material possessions and he was focused on accumulating as much as possible. As he held on to his ownership as the most valuable and precious jewel, he also harbored the fear of losing his possessions. This fear did not allow George to share. Even if he did share, his sharing came out of fear, and hence his fear taught him to become selfish and egotistical.

He lived and breathed for his possessions. It was all about what and how much he had. It was important for his image in society. He needed to be accepted and appreciated by others for what he possessed. He desired to stand on his high podium to receive the recognition, praise and respect from others. And all these false desires made him acquire the notion of superiority and control, all the while as Lucia got suffocated and abused.

His ego was all about taking; and he never had enough! He was always shopping for new ideas, new things, and new concepts. His ego was never satisfied, never happy, never fulfilled. It was always about "I, me, and mine". His egotistical and ambitious race kept destroying all that is beautiful, a wonderful life that could have flowered and become a peak of his existence.

The only way to tame the nature of George's false Self or ego would be to turn inward, turn to God. He needed to spend time in silence, in prayer, in meditation, in contemplation. A great discipline is required to attain peace, harmony and joy. Praying to our Lord is the only way to freedom.

Both George and Lucia cannot live without God. They delude themselves into thinking that they alone can reach to the heavenly gates. While in reality, they are way too weak for such a major undertaking.

They always need God in their life! They need His guidance, His support, His accompaniment! Only through Him can they learn to know themselves, their path, their purpose, and their truth!

There is no greater reward and greater freedom than knowing who they are so that they can live a meaningful and peaceful life. And the effort is necessary. They have to make all efforts that are possible. No energy should be left unused. They must get involved and work as a unit. Only then achievement and flowering will be possible.

But can fear sometimes work wonders too? Yes it can! And it did! I will tell you exactly what happened to George and what effect fear had on him.

GEORGE'S TURNAROUND

Exactly one day before Lucia was suppose to return home from her retreat, George had a vivid and very powerful dream which he will long remember. It was a profound reminder that triggered his deeper contemplation and repentance.

In the dream, George was wandering around the city, seemingly without any purpose. As he walked down the street, he noticed a beggar sitting on the sidewalk. His clothes were old and torn, his long hair all tufted, and his poorly groomed beard hung below his chest. He was old and his body looked fragile and weak.

As George came closer to the beggar, he leaned over him and mockingly asked how much money he needed. The beggar did not answer his query and instead handed a piece of rolled up paper to

George and told him to take it and read it. George cynically smiled, turning his head with the intention to walk away. But the beggar was persistent and urged him to take the paper and told him that he would not repent.

George took the paper and put it in his pocket. He took two steps then turned around to throw another look of disapproval towards the beggar. To his alarm, he noticed that the old man was no longer there!

George's eyes widened in uncertainty; his gaze scanned the crowd in search of the mysterious beggar. He could not spot him anywhere, and thought to himself; How could a man disappear like that in just a blink of an eye?! It was absolutely impossible. He was too weak and too old to vanish so quickly and so easily.

George remained in the same place a few more minutes, still astonished about the mysterious disappearance of the beggar, unsure of what just happened! Now curious, he pulled out the paper from his pocket, unrolled it and saw only one sentence written on it that said, 'I was exactly like YOU and realized it only after I died!'

George was in an absolute shock; he did not know what to think. Great confusion entered his psyche and it seemed that the fear of death was penetrating his very bones. He did not want to die. He wanted to run away and hide. He felt as though he was receiving a severe beating on his head. Suddenly he started sweating uncontrollably. His thoughts were swirling around ferociously. His whole being shook as leaves on an autumn day. His chest got tight, prompting him to jump out of bed to gasp for air.

Still confused and scared to death, he could not sleep for the rest of the night. He pondered deeply about his dream; the dream that seemed so real, so convincing and striking. The dream that would cause quite a turnaround in George's forthcoming thinking. It served as a twist towards other realizations when his psychological thoughts would gradually thin out and allow him to be more patient, loving, and understanding.

George had always been against poverty and often exhorted Lucia to make efforts to acquire more and to be less generous. At the same time, deep in his being, George was equally propitious and giving. As a child he was always modest and did not think about material gain. Like many of the other children he wasn't lacking in anything. The kids all had their essential environmental necessities. Of course there were difficulties in the village and people occasionally struggled, but the entire community remained brave and resourceful. When George would hear people complain about material issues it bothered him to some extent, but he would give it more thought and come to realize there was no need to fear. He would tell his father; 'Dad, don't worry. When I grow up I will work and help you'. The other rural kids would say the same to their parents. No matter how small and immature they were, they obviously all felt the parental difficulties, and George was not an exception.

While George watched and listened to people complain and fear death, he shrugged it off. This was not his fear, but he cultivated other fears deep within him. A fear that had long festered inside of him was the fear of poverty. He also lived in constant fear of not being good enough and sufficiently obedient. He was afraid of punishment. George had a big mouth and often said out loud what others would not dare say. Even if he spoke the truth, adults didn't tolerate these kind of things.

He feared mother's spankings because each time she did he would literally faint. He would also pass out if a male shouted at him. Eventually adults all knew the situation and were more careful. His mother used to say; ' Unfortunately I can't spank anymore, even though it's deserved on many occasions'.

He was afraid to go to church confessional and lay bare his sins. He always kept a few to himself. He was afraid the priest would betray him and tell others of his failures. The confessional space itself also caused him some discomfort. He didn't like confined spaces with only one tiny opening with a screen. The fact that he could not clearly see the priest's eyes also felt unnatural and spooky.

He was passionately afraid of one of the teachers at school who would beat children like cattle using hand, foot, and rod. He couldn't stand this ugly behavior and the harsh words used on his pupils. Every time the teacher entered the classroom George felt fear and disgust in his stomach. The whole village knew what kind of teacher their kids had, yet nobody did anything about it. He taught at the school for many years and no one said a word.

George did not have much trust in love. Watching some rural husbands disrespect and abuse their wives gave him the impression that love is hurtful and is far from the beauty of love in the lyrics of songs.

But George's greatest fear was his fear of God. He thought God was the most powerful force: a force only used to threaten and punish. George's vision of God was that of an all-powerful being sitting in a heavenly garden: observing who thinks what, who says what, who does what, and allocating punishments accordingly. He couldn't believe that

God is love, and thus George never felt His proximity.

All rural kids learned about hell at a very young age. They knew that if they were not good and not obedient, God would cast them to eternal fire from which it was impossible to escape. The Holy purgatory seemed to suit the children much better as punishment. Sure this punishment also had some flames for purification, but at least this place was only temporary.

George was also afraid for Lucia because he thought that she was too quiet, too good, too emotional, too trusty, too weak, and too naive. He feared that others might exploit and cheat her. He wanted her to be an extrovert; loud and strong, expressing any thought with no care of what others might say.

Lucia, on the other hand, did not have any of these fears. She always felt that her childhood was colored by perfection. Lucia was Lucia; even if she had something to say, who would hear her and listen?

Regardless of his fears, much of George's adult life was spent aspiring to be successful and his energy put towards realizing his many dreams. Doing so made him successful. Yet having earned his business and achieved his several aspirations, it still seemed that he was not fully satisfied. He often felt that there was something missing in his life and he did not know what it was. He was constantly looking, searching, shopping, calculating, and analyzing: hopping from one objective to the next and never feeling satisfied with the results. Whenever he received something that he deemed was not enough; he would go on asking for more and complaining about his slim pickings. He was obsessed with his thoughts and he was too occupied in questioning. He did not know that questioning in and of itself was often pointless. Of course there are a few significant questions worth spending the time contemplating: but for these, the answer often comes through silence, peace, trust, patience and receptivity. George was incapable of these qualities. He was restless, edgy and impatient. He would not go through the discipline of asking receptively. He was more concerned with formulating the questions. Even when the answer was given to him, he would move on to another question, and he would actually create many more questions out of the answer itself. Questions would keep coming out of him as leaves grow on a tree, like forest mushrooms appear after a heavy rain. And he was never satisfied with a small amount of questions. He wanted to question everything and he wanted to know everything. But he never asked the one and only real fundamental question: 'who am I'. Even if he did, he would be unprepared to receive and understand the answer. His unstable nature would never allow him such a finding because this question is unanswerable. Any answer that

George's memory gave him would not be of any use. The real answer would have to come from his innermost self and this is not the same. He would need to keep asking this question over and over again, and any answer that would appear from his memories would need to slowly drop away. And once he was empty of these answers and only the question remained, then this same question would take him inward to where it would collapse upon itself and a state of emptiness would take over. It is in this state of emptiness, where this question 'who am I' does not arise anymore, that miracles happen.

Lucia, on the other hand, did not have any questions. In her world there was only the answer, because Lucia knew how not to ask, how to be patient, how to trust, or how to wait. Her subtle knowing and wisdom let the whole existence be, and she never interrupted its being. She let the sun rise, she let the river flow, she let the storm rush, she let the rainfall, she let the wind blow, she let the spring arrive by itself. She was never upset or disappointed, and her world was full of childlike admiration and wonder. She let reality flow and allowed perplexity to exist without questioning it. Lucia had her own way of seeing, perceiving and understanding the mystery of life. All that is beautiful, meaningful, joyful and significant sprouts was in her garden. It is in her soil that love, compassion, gratitude and spirit grew. Without Lucia, George would not know the beauty of feeling and joy of loving. George is a warrior, but he is not a lover. He could not know poetry and painting without Lucia. Nor would he know the value of prayer and the power of heavenly Grace. Lucia was a master! The throne belonged to her but she never bothered to claim it. She had no need to prove herself and therefore, she let George pretend to be a master even though he was meant to be a servant. She let George think that he knew best, and she knew that George was a creation of the ancient rural society; that his education originated from the majority; and that his thinking was no different than that of the rest of the people in the village. He is as smart and clever as others, but he could not see that every being has its individuality and uniqueness. Of course it is always good to listen, to learn and participate in flock, but it's important to see that it is not always as others claim. He often failed to follow his own individual drive, and this hampered him on his path to freedom. It had taken him quite a long time to see how deep his beautiful being was buried under myriad lies.

Lucia stood by George's side and helped at every opportunity. She was persistent in her intention and kept him carefully and firmly in her vicinity. She was determined to show him the path to his true essence. Although he tried to escape on many occasions during the process towards Self-realization, she never gave up. How could she? She knew that this was their most significant lifetime goal.

With her persistent help and effort, George learned the power of prayer and meditation. He gradually adopted the skill to relax and be in the moment. As this awareness of prayer and rest began to penetrate his being, he felt as if a big block of ice was melting away. Layers of his false identity started peeling off and disappearing. He was clearly recognizing his conditioned habits and barriers, and from this space slowly rose silence and peace. By and by George gained greater strength, serenity and joy. His creativity started spontaneously emerging. He began to draw various images of nature and painting with oil on canvas as a welcome expression of his fresh new vision. Even as his hands, face, and clothes were completely smeared with oils, he did not care as he giggled like a child and he enjoyed every moment. He felt inspired like when he was a child. He was reminded of when he was young, kneading clay in the summer; he played with clay and created a variety of interesting pieces, including the holy family that he left in the sun to dry. He later placed it all in a box which he kept until the Christmas holidays to lay under the Christmas tree. What a beautiful memory!

As time went by George was able to recognize that love is not a poetic event but a reality of significant value: that Love is the way, and that the way is loving intelligence. He became aware that when love and intelligence meet together they create a space in which all is plausible. If intelligence is alone, it dries and stays immaterial. When love is alone, it is sentiment and unrealized. The blend is absolutely necessary, and the combination of intellect and wisdom transforms iron into jewels.

This awareness gave George a new kind of integrity and a new flight. He understood that with true love, clear intelligence and trust would come real freedom. And freedom was the ultimate desire in both, George and Lucia. The freedom of their inner meadow was the only true freedom; only in that freedom could they flourish, could they celebrate, could they dance, could they sing, could they play, could they invent, could they create!

I love and respect both my heart and mind - Lucia and George. They deserve my immense praise and great recognition for their every effort. It is irrelevant to me that one is servant and the other is master. To me they both deserve the royal seat; a throne that signifies great love, respect and integrity. Even though I love them infinitely, I am neither George nor Lucia. They are only my instruments. They live in my house and I am their landlord. Or are they actually my servants and I am their master? Yes, I am a master that allows them to work as they want and I do not interfere in their business. Their business is not mine. My only duty is to observe them, watch them. I simply remain as a witness and look where these roommates are going. George is going one way and Lucia is going another way because they are different. In fact they are diametrically opposite; they are incompatible and inconsistent. I am not to be a follower of them. I am not to identify with them. If I did, they would mislead me and take me to ruin, because as much as George can be dangerous in certain areas, Lucia can also stumble through all kinds of imaginations, hallucinations, illusions, and sweet dreams. Neither of them can give me truth. The truth is behind the coming together of both George and Lucia while in my consciousness and awareness. It is my consciousness that holds the absolute truth; it is separate from them and it can use them both harmoniously.

Therefore I am simply to abide as a watcher and watch them move and explore. Right or wrong, I am to see it as a great experience. An experience where I am neither George nor Lucia. I simply remain behind them. I am merely observing. If I interfere and get identified with them, they cannot go anywhere, as they do not have their own energy. My consciousness is their only source of vital force. It is the space where everything originates, appears, and manifests in both their inner and outer worlds. Their life could not exist without my consciousness, so therefore my consciousness is the only authentic master and keeper of the ultimate truth. My only duty is to watch and observe both George and Lucia without identifying with them.

However, as much as George and Lucia are my instruments and servants and I their watcher, I am also a servant. I am a servant in the form of a person who serves my consciousness. Therefore all three of us are playing the role of service to the consciousness in the form of a triangle.

We all live relatively; we think, we feel, we express, we do, we enjoy, and we serve the higher consciousness. But I still predominantly remain as an observer and watch where George and Lucia are going and what they are doing. Because that is the only way that they can find their mutual inner and outer peace; coming to agreement and becoming as a single instrument producing sweet notes and melodies. Nevertheless all three of us simultaneously must have a desire to serve, to know, and to realize our higher consciousness: our higher Being. For time will come when the triangle that the three of us formed will melt into the power of higher consciousness. Melt into the power of the Supreme Being. And when this moment comes, all three of us will become emptiness; a void in which our Supreme Being will reveal itself and allow us to realize our Self. It will serve as a mirror to all three of us that we are That, and we could never be anything else.

Until we reach this point, Lucia will keep reminding George what to do and how to be in order to find out who they truly are. She will gradually teach him how to observe every phenomenal object, be it inner and outer, without associating with it. And I will remain as an observer of both George and Lucia: without any identification regarding what they are thinking, what they are speaking, and what they are doing.

RECONCILIATION

When Lucia returned home from the retreat, she found George at home in an unexpected spirit of joy. She could not believe her eyes and to her surprise George had taken a month off from work and planned to spend the whole time with her.

George sincerely apologized to Lucia and promised that he would never disrespect her again. He also stated that he was now more open than ever before and ready to do whatever Lucia wanted him to do.

Lucia was glowing with appreciation and dropped the issues they had been arguing about before. She requested that he be a true seeker of his inner truth, and hold within himself a deep desire to awaken from the delusion of his ego.

Lucia began,

"You must know that we are one and the same reality.

We were born under the same roof and came through the same parents.

They baptized us with the same love countless times.

They warmed us to the same fire, bathed us, and quenched our thirst.

They fed us and taught us the Ten Commandments equally.

Their prayers became our own.

We felt their desires and joys; we shed their tears of sorrow.

We discerned their ongoing efforts for the sake of belonging.

Their sense of unknowing the truth of existence, became our bondage.

We must break the chain of our ignorance by realizing what we are not.

We must meet each other without our thoughts, without our conditioning.

Our meeting must take a place in the depths of our being, the only place we can both relax and just be.

I am aware that we can be thinking geniuses, but our thoughts will never allow us to taste enlightenment.

We must be liberated for all this.

We must free ourselves from our troubled thoughts and our Self-projected hardships.

Our ego is hurting us in many different ways, and we must become aware of it.

Our ego is creating our own suffering.

Deep down in our being, we are crying for liberation, but we do not know it.

How many nights we could not sleep in peace?
Why do you think that is?

How many times did we experience panic attacks?
Where do you think that comes from?

Not from our practical thoughts my beloved, our
practical thinking has nothing to do with our
suffering.

It is our psychological properties, our ego-thinking
my love!

Whatever we think and imagine ourselves to be,
we are not.

Whatever we think we have, we do not.

We do not need to ask why, since we do not need
to know.

Our thoughts can not answer that question, only
our inner being can realize it through prayers,
through silence.

The only question we should ask is, 'who am I'?

To firmly hold on to that question and contemplate on it, meditate on it, be with it.

Let's, together, feel it deeply in our being.

Let's find out 'who am I' and let it be our daily mantra: our ongoing prayer.

Let it be the flow of our precious blood. Let it be carried by the main artery of our being.

We need to be in silence and calmness to feel it and perceive it.

We cannot break it open by force.

We need to stand still, my beloved. It needs to be done by the inner will-

We must free ourselves from this slavery. We must liberate ourselves from our deep-seated ignorance.

For so many years, we overlooked the obvious and the basic fact of life.

We had no understanding of our inner power.

We could not realize it sooner.

We were blind.

Nobody ever pointed it out to us, they could not have.

We borrowed their knowledge but their knowledge is not our wisdom.

Our wisdom comes from within our being, from our own experiences.

We must become strong, wise and awakened.

Do you remember anybody in the village that spoke about Self-realization?

They did not. They could not.

They did not know what it meant.

All of them like us, went to church every Sunday and they were good and decent people but could not recognize their true inner power.

They, like us, probably thought that God was far away and impossible to reach.

A long trip and many sacrifices were required to get close to Him.

It is not how often we had been to church; it is about accepting Christ as our Lord and Savior and to create an intimate relationship with God.

Only through deep love we can establish that reality.

There is no greater vision, no greater understanding, than love.

But we were afraid of love, we were afraid of God.

To us God was a threatening and a dangerous authority!

As kids, even a simple thunder was a significant sign of God's disappointment.

When the thick dark clouds began gathering and closing the sky over the village, we felt some discomfort and fear, even before the thunder started shooting down on the earth.

Every time lightning would strike, adults would tell us,

'You better be good, God is coming down to get you.'

We believed them!"

George jumps up to speak,

"I remember an occasion during a thunderstorm where we ran as fast as we could to get home and when we arrived and found that our parents were absent we felt even more afraid.

We ran into the kitchen searching for a safe hideout and decided to cower under the kitchen table.

But soon we felt that it was not safe enough because the kitchen window had no blinds.

We could hear the thunder and see the lightning pierce through the window and come right through.

So, during a short break in the storm, we ran to our bedroom to hide under our beds.

But getting there we realized there was a huge pile of potatoes packed underneath.

We had to take them out from under the bed; dispersing the potatoes all over the bedroom floor to make some space so we could crawl under and wait for the thunder to pass."

INTERVAL

Lucia knew precisely how they felt but George had no idea that the whole process of looking into the past together was to see and learn from it as one.

George usually recollects rather troubling issues and has difficulty releasing them so bad memories are prone to occupy his psyche longer.

This subject was hard on George and so Lucia decided to give him a break and asked him if he had a special memory of any particular season in the village. He gladly replied and said it was autumn!

He continued,

"I was so happy in the autumn season, and could not wait for it to arrive.

Harvesting grapes was the main reason.

The whole process of grape harvesting and clusters crushing was so exhilarating and fun to me.

I remember the vineyards echoed with the songs that the people sang.

Everyone was overjoyed from experiencing such a rich season.

Some would sort the grape clusters and put them into buckets, while others would carry the clusters to the end of the vineyard

where they would dump the buckets into a flat wide barrel for young girls to press with their bare feet.

It seemed to me as if the young girls were dancing some fiery and magical dance, holding their dress with one hand while the other hand held to the edge of the barrel. Their Dance transforming the clusters into a young wine."

George goes on,

"I remember when the villagers could not wait
until the complex process of must was finished so
they could taste the wine.

For the villagers this was a moment as important
as the celebration of church holidays. This was
usually in the month of November on St. Martin's
day."

St. Martin's feast is a wine baptism ritual
celebrated since the seventeenth century and
mostly in the northern parts of Croatia.

Priest Martin, who was allegedly a true lover of
wine, started this playful baptizing ritual.

In the ritual of baptism, actresses would dress up
and take on the roles of judges, bishops,
godmothers, and godfathers of the wine.

This marry company praised the God of wine in witty prayers to give their host an abundance of food and gallons of good wine.

"Wine was and still is their favorite drink. There is nothing like it.

A drop of wine was called a drop of health.

It seemed they could not live without it.

They drank every day, often not just a glass or two but liters!

They drank it like water from a village well.

Wine gave them strength and joy and made them forget their troubles.

Wine was indeed their most significant gift-

Do you remember in winter when the village men would get together and drink their wine?

They would visit different homes on different days and gather around the hearth full of fire, where they kept toasting, drinking and singing their patriotic songs late into the night.

They would feel joyous and relaxed and often drunk to the point that some of them would have a hard time getting home.

Their patriotic songs often stirred up their emotions and made them drink more.

They would sing those songs every time they'd get together even though they were not allowed to sing them.

The former communist government forbade people to sing their patriotic songs or say anything against the alleged law.

Village people had to be very careful who was listening when they sang or spoke something against communist state.

If the administration found out, those people were punished.

People could not say a word against the regime. The police would often come to the village for no other reason than to verify that no one was offending the government.

Croatian people as a whole did not have this freedom for that matter.

Many Croatian people moved because of this. Some immigrated legally while others, as refugees.

Even if they moved out of the country, they still did not have freedom as long as the communist regime was alive. They were still monitored and followed by the communist spies throughout the world, wherever the Croats settled.

Apparently, their spies would stop by Croatian churches and centers around the world where people would meet and gather.

So in that, Montreal was no different. Croats had, and still have, their church and center where they go regularly.

The door is wide open to anyone who wants to come and pray or celebrate different occasions at the center.

Since the communist police would freely come in and join any Croatians gathering, they could hear who sang patriotic songs or who spoke against their state. They would also have documented the culprits and later report them to the government.

If the culprits went back to visit their homeland, police waited for them at the border and took them away to prison.

For this reason some Croatians could not even visit their loved ones who were left behind when they moved away from home.

Many of who remained imprisoned and often tortured for alleged crimes against the government.

All that finally changed when the Croatian people gained their independence. This was a difficult path. It was not simple for them to face communism and its military force.

However, who knows how long the peace will last?"

Lucia then said,

"Please do not say that, everything is as it should be, everything is perfect.

Today Croatian people live better than ever before. The blue Adriatic is now open and accessible to everyone. They have gained from opening up its borders to the world and tourism has flourished. The world can finally taste the beauty of Croatia."

PLUNGING DEEPER

Lucia comes back to the main subject but George seems a little hesitant and scared. Indeed, he had previously mentioned that he feared getting lost in the process of Self-discovery.

Lucia is very much aware of his pain since his thoughts are still as sharp as a spear; piercing his psyche and not allowing him peace.

He is not yet inclined to watch his thoughts, to simply witness them and get familiar with their nature. Yet Lucia does not worry for she knows that this will come later.

Lucia continues with the subject and says,

"Our words are not important, my beloved.

What is important is listening. We need to hear our inner voice, from the deep silence, from the bottom of our being.

We can not constantly run and search for happiness through the possessions we acquire even if we know they have value in many happy returns.

But they won't bring us permanent joy since they are only a temporary high.

Once they lose their shine we will again search new ventures to seek and never find everlasting delight.

External forces will never fulfill us, my beloved; permanent treasure lies only in the depths of our being, awaiting for us to discover it.

We must learn to live in the moment joyfully and playfully.

Our intelligence must grow younger and sharper, our love higher and deeper.

Truth can not be found in the outside world, for it is within us.

Let's seek our truth with our own company. Let's be ourselves.

We can not get lost by realizing the Self, we can get lost by never realizing it.

But you have to promise me that you will work with me side by side.

So we can acknowledge who we are not, so we become aware of who we truly are.

Our phenomenal existence is superficial; it is make-believe.

We do not know our existence but God does. He is asking of us to be the being we are, the being He created us to be and to never try to be another.

His power fashioned our own individuality, our uniqueness, so we could express it on the stage of our physical existence in the most meaningful way.

Let's be mature and wise. Wisdom is accepting the responsibility of being who we are: focusing and unifying our awareness.

We must not get distracted by external fleeting joy. We must remain in our knowing.

Our knowledge belongs to the past.

Our knowing belongs to us, to our present moment, to our consciousness.

There is no ready-made path. It does not come cheap.

It needs our faithful devotion to God to attain our ultimate truth.

We must risk it all to be ourselves.

We did not come to this planet accidentally. We are here by design, meaningfully and for a reason.

We have a commitment to life. Some important message has to be delivered through us. Some significant work has to be completed through us."

George now has watery eyes which means he is trusting Lucia. He is opening to learn more, allowing Lucia to continue.

Lucia continues,

"Our intuition is the key to our consciousness.

We must contemplate on our consciousness and keep quiet to feel it.

To trust in it fully.

To realize that our consciousness is our very essence, our true religion.

It is in our innermost being.

It is the space in our center ever present and alive.

It never changes and never dies.

It is simply imperishable, it is indescribable.

Let's stay with it, let's look at it.

Let's see it, let's feel it, let's taste it.

We must keep persevering and training ourselves to look inward.

Let's make this a habit.

This is done by ignoring the external forces and moving in the silence of our inner force.

Let's just relax and be.

Let's not expect anything, let's not wait for something to happen.

We should let the sound of silence envelope our being, to stay in the depth of our innermost reality.

Let's feel it deeply, it is by feeling it that we will realize it.

To remain in that space of our ever living consciousness.

Let's stay in that flame of our knowing.

Let's meditate on that flame.

Let's relax in that flame.

Let's become that burning inner flame."

Lucia now notices George's exhaustion, and proposes to take a break and change the subject. She asks George if he remembers the time when as kids they learned about racism right next to home in the village.

"Of course I do", George instantly replied and started,

"There was a young girl in our village who later moved to the city with her parents. During her stay in the city, she met an African boy who came to Croatia as a student and wanted to study at Croatian university.

The two met and came to know each other very well and eventually fell in love and got married.

A few years later, she returned to the village with her husband and her daughter to visit her grandfather.

When they arrived the rural people certainly had something to talk about. No one in the region ever had a black person visit their village."

George continues,

"They all ran and gathered around this family to see them up close and kept their eyes fixated on her husband and daughter.

The villagers did not even notice the girl who grew up in their village and whom they had not seen for years. Instead their all of their attention was devoted to the two black people!

After the girl and her family left for her grandpa's house, they all started laughing and gossiping: and this lasted for quite a while.

The village folks could not understand why their girl did not choose one of their village boys, and instead decided to marry a black foreigner."

Now Lucia will tell where this story originates from.

"Allegedly many years ago, the grandfather of this girl worked as a sailor on a foreign ship.

He was the only one in the village at the time who ventured from home and travelled that far.

He worked long and hard hours. He did not take any time off for two years!

He wanted to stay and work as much as possible and earn as much money that he could.

In the village there was hard labor as well, but no money.

As a sailor, the grandfather sailed the seas and saw many beautiful places in the world, and he met many interesting people.

Apparently Africa and their people were his favorite!

He passionately loved that part of the world and talked about it all the time.

After a while he had to stop working on the ship because he suffered from severe asthma.

During the summer, he sat in the shade of trees, telling stories to the village children. He rarely spoke to adults.

He enjoyed recounting the many tales from his travels around the world.

One of these stories was about African people and their nature.

He said that African men reminded him a lot of Croatian men from Dalmatian area. They are as tall and handsome. They liked to drink, sing and take it easy like Dalmatians.

He spoke to the children about slavery and what the African people had gone through; often tearing up himself as he felt their pain.

He also told the children that in Africa people always sang, and that their songs were both their joy and their salvation. He would say, "Freedom can be taken from a man but his spirit remains intact."

This man was truly in love with Africa and would often say

that he would much rather live in any African village than in his own.

He must have gone to his grave happy knowing that his granddaughter enjoyed part of his dream."

INQUIRE

Lucia is curious what George has to tell about their entire discussion so far,

"What do you think about everything that we talked about and did you at least learn something?"

George responds,

"I don't think I learned anything other than the idea that I can reduce Earth's 7 billion people to the 150 souls who used to live in the village, and by doing so I get a glimpse of everyone's reality for an entire globe.

Whatever was going on in the village back then serves as a mirror of whole world; a world that is full of poverty, lies, and wars.

A world that has never had and never will have justice."

Lucia is deeply touched by George's comments and says,

"I hear you my beloved and I understand you completely.

But we need to learn that we can not change people.

We cannot change the world.

It is not possible to do so.

Actually, our world is not different from the rest of the world.

We constantly lie to ourselves and tell ourselves that we are what we are not. In doing so we steal from ourselves truth and freedom because we are not who we think we are.

We are manipulating ourselves by thinking that our assets are a reflection of our world, when in reality our consciousness is the true representation.

We are often at war because we are not able to find mutual understanding, peace and happiness. War is not in the world but in us.

The only way we can change the world is by changing ourselves.

The best way to contribute to the world is by realizing who we are.

Our Self-realization is the way, it is Self-love.

We know life and death but we do not know awakening.

Our deep inner knowing is waiting for us to awaken.

We must lift the veil of our blindness and we must destroy our unawareness.

We must not allow our descendants to suffer for the sake of our ignorance for they do not deserve that kind of punishment.

They can inherit all our material but those assets won't help them learn the meaning of human maturity and the maturity of their spirit.

We must sow the power of wisdom so that they could reap the benefits of peace and the joy of a meaningful and prosperous life.

But teaching begins at the altar of our own home, as it must be a role model for them and many future generations to come.

Our ancestors taught us to be aware of deadly sins because committing these acts could cascade and affect blood relatives up to the fourth generation. What they did not teach us was that our ignorance is one of our greatest sins and the cause of all our hardships.

When we are unaware our actions become sins, regardless of whether we live and act in a state of sleep.

Unless we direct our consciousness to a higher plane of understanding and awakening, our actions will remain useless and there won't be any value in them.

We should not focus on what our ancestors gave us or did not give us. They gave us what they could and knew.

Now it is up to us to create a better life and to know that it is

not only about the journey, but also about the destination with God.

St Francis said: "What you are looking for is already where you are looking from."

Hence, the travelling is not necessary to find who we are, but the destination is. It is right here in our being, in our consciousness, the place beyond journeying, beyond all the memories, beyond every object, beyond every imagination, beyond every question and every answer.

Doubt, for doubt is not a sin. It is a sign of our intelligence.

But we need to let the world be as it is.

We can not let the past haunt us and the future dissuade us.

The past no longer exists and the future has not yet arrived.

As long as we live in the memories of the past, we do not really live.

We're missing on life.

We do not belong to memories and time. We belong to eternity.

Let's take hold of our own life my beloved.

We are not here to attain life, we are life.

Our life is not a thing; it is a process; it is a natural stream without end, it is consciousness that was never born and never dies.

Our life is poetry to be written; it is a melody to be composed, it is a prance to be danced; it is a lyric to be sung.

Let's see that all of existence is moving and flowing like a river without end.

These trees in the forest are vigorous, radiant and cheerful.

These birds are sweet and joyous.

The lakes, rivers and oceans bathe in their wild.

Animals are careless, playful, and happy in their world.

The whole earth is swaying in the infinite splendor of delight and beauty.

The eternal orchestra of life is playing and celebrating all over the world.

We must not be afraid my beloved.

Our whole life we lived in fear.

We feared the known, we feared the unknown.

We had a fear of death. We had a fear of hell.

We feared of never reaching the heaven.

We feared of not making our stamp in the world and being nobody.

We are not to become followers of fear. We have to face it and fight it.

The more fear we have in us, the less opportunity for our Self-realization and freedom.

Our life should be enveloped by love, by peace, and by harmony. Not by fear.

Our psychological thoughts are our fear and conditioning.

We should not identify with our thoughts.

We should not judge them nor argue with them.

We can watch them.

Our thoughts are not even ours as they operate as a unifying force of society.

We should look at them from our inner space and witness them, but let them flow as water in the riverbed.

Let them come and let them go.

Our thoughts have no roots.

They can not stay, they are only visitors.

They have no power to occupy our dwelling.

They are floating around like clouds in the sky.

We must get familiar with them and get close to them.

Let's invite them over and see what happens.

They won't be able to disturb us.

They come around but have no power to remain.

They can not since our home is not their destination.

We need to become aware of our consciousness.

Our consciousness is our master key to happiness.

It will open the door to our freedom.

It is always here and it will forever be.

Our consciousness does not need anything to be beautified.

It does not need ornaments.

It does not require any of our thinking nor any perception of our conditioning or control.

It needs our vast and profound devotion to higher existence.

We are part of Christ's consciousness but we must rise to understand that.

We must surrender to God and his Almighty power to know our inner truth.

We must be naked to realize who we are.

We must move beyond the person and personal predispositions and acknowledge the power of our ever-living awareness.

When we move from our person-hood back to our consciousness, we take a great recognition of Self, a being that is meant to be and act as an instrument of coexistence with Supreme Being. In doing so the whole cosmic energy becomes available to us.

When we operate only from our limited point of view, our awareness is reduced, stagnated, and constrained. Our space is narrowed and inadequate.

So let's move beyond our personal attitude into the state of our inspirational authenticity so that we can think, speak, and work from our true place.

Let's realize the Self my beloved!

Let's be and serve as an evidence that God exists!"

George was looking for an escape and said,

"I'm scared! I'm scared of change! What if I realize the truth and I don't like it?

What if I can't come back to who I'm now. Can we postpone it!"

Lucia got firm in her conviction and continued,

"We do not have time to waste my beloved.

We can not possibly keep coming back from one life to the next.

We need to realize the Self in this lifetime, and we need to realize it now while we are still warm. While we are still alive.

We must wake up from the slumber of our delusion into a bright space of pure awareness: the simple truth which will set us free from sorrow and confusion."

FRUIT HARVEST

Lucia kept pointing out to George what needs to be done in order for them to realize who they are. They did absolutely everything that was possible to do to attain their freedom. They learned to keep quiet, avoid the influence of thoughts, abide in self, and keep observing. George still had many questions but over time he realized that the questions and answers did not have any value. This was because both questions and answers were emerging from his memory and not from his inner flower. In the end only one question remained; the question, 'who am I'? This question became George's and Lucia's center stage; they invested all their energy in it and it seemed as if every cell of their being screamed out for this answer. After asking many times and after all answers had collapsed, they no longer even had the question. The question 'who am I' took them inward where the question itself had fallen away and it did not arise anymore. At this point they did not have any question nor did they have anything left to observe. A state of silence penetrated their being tremendously. The fruits of their labor had become ripe and the harvest was in progress.

This happened one early evening while George and Lucia were sitting on the couch with no thoughts and no words; each immersed in their own world. Although they are by nature two completely different worlds, at this point it was obvious to see that they beautifully merged into one; as a restful flower and its alluring fragrance. There was no one millimeter spacing between them and the following moment they started melting which caused the two sides of the triangle completely disappear.

And with that I, as an observer of George and Lucia also had nothing left to observe. The screen of my perception became completely empty which meant the rest of the triangle was about to crush together. All the while a higher consciousness or a higher Being was and is constantly present. Whatever was going on in our life this pure awareness perceived and observed it all from its imperishable and inexhaustible source in which the whole existence irrigates and manifests itSelf. This same space is also located within our innermost being, open and accessible for Self-discovery.

Since George and Lucia melted in the power of peace and harmony it was now my personality's turn to surrender in arms of a higher consciousness or source. Most of my identity at this point has already disappeared along with George and Lucia because their sublime unity has caused also my personal identity to start to melt away. In this state the door of a higher consciousness was opened which previously could not happen because George's ego was standing at the mouth of freedom. His quite crystallized ego and pride was preventing both himself and Lucia from passing over the threshold of their highest truth. Although I as a personal identity allowed it to be so because I previously identified with the power of George's ego which was only an idea and not reality. His ego did not have any substance but I strongly believed that it did.

However as my identity was disappearing I have become absolutely alone; without George, Lucia, or my personality. I was becoming nothing and nobody and this state of presence was allowing my naked being to experience greater reality. Because in the following moments only profound peace and dense silence was present. As I sat on the couch in the deep calm and tranquility in the coming moments I no longer saw the difference between my being and the interior space of my home. I was merging with the space and becoming one with it. And this time it all became overwhelming that I started gasping for air. I got up from the couch with the intention to rush for the door and get outside but soon realized that my footsteps became quite stiff. And in that instant I felt as if I heard a voice or maybe a thought that said, "don't move"- I sat back on the couch and felt my whole head becoming numb. I wanted to rush again to stand up and say something but I could not stand up nor could I say a single word. And suddenly like a speed of light, like a storm, took over my being completely and shook my foundation to its roots. It seemed the whole universe was spinning around me. It felt so powerful and real; I thought that was the end of me. I panicked but not for too long. I somehow knew that this had to be done; for the sake of my highest truth, for the sake of my freedom. I surrendered-

Shortly after the whole storm subsided but my head remained completely numb and suspended. I had no single thought to think. My lips were seemingly stuck closed. I could not pronounce anything. Something had completely emptied me from myself. Everything seemed so transparent and light. It felt that I could walk through the walls although I could barely move.

Eventually I managed to get to my bed; lay down and stayed awake as an absolute emptiness, bound and motionless. Even my eyelids did not bother to blink: I peered into an endless void. The sound of silence was so rich and thick that it was nearly tangible. And in that stillness time had completely stopped. There was no yesterday or tomorrow. Everything merged into timelessness. At some point I felt the space like a mother's womb, warm, comfortable and loving; no thoughts, no words, no fear, no time, only pure presence in which I remained awake all night long. Actually I was not the one who was awake, there was only the awakening.

The following morning I fell asleep for a few hours; when I woke up I realized that my speech returned. And also some of my thoughts began to slowly emerge but nowhere near what they used to be. Later on, it became clear to me that all psychological thoughts no longer had any place in the house. They had simply vanished. But for some reason the sound of OM appeared in my head and remained constantly present for several months. I would hear it continuously and sometimes much more pronounced especially while writing and describing my deeper feelings. The sound would be almost unbearable, so much that I'd have to take a break.

My body also had become weak and heavy. I had no pain but I was barely moving and felt as if I was an old lady. It took about four months for my physical strength to return. In the meantime I wrote and received a deeper understanding of the experience and confirmed that George's ego was indeed the only obstacle to the awakening. As with the disappearance of his ego there was no longer any concern, worry or anguish. George got completely liberated from his psychological thoughts and gained a new and fresh intelligence, knowledge and understanding. While Lucia has deepened her wisdom, love and compassion. Their devotion and loyalty towards the eternal consciousness and God granted us the most precious jewel of humanity. We continue harmoniously live, serve, share, and honor this immortal Truth for as long as we remain in this mortal body. Although, I am still neither George nor Lucia; I am beyond both. I am consciousness itSelf, and so are you, and so is every being as we can not be anything else. We only need to realize It. As with the experience of awakening or Self-realization peace, joy and contentment becomes the evidence that everything is as it should be and that all moves in an enormous power of intelligence and harmony. There is not a thing to change or fix as I know nothing except that God exists. Whereas within me a single question did not remain. However, once I wondered 'is this is enough honor and gratitude one could pledge on the Altar of Divinity?'

'Yes', the voice whispered within my being- 'Yes, and be certain to keep declaring your love for Him! For what you realized can not be for a single season'…

I dedicate this book to my children Sandra and Josip Lerga in the hope that they wake up and realize their highest truth in this lifetime since this is my fundamental desire and love for them. I hold the same aspiration for the rest of my family near and far. Also for all the believers and seekers who wish to discover this simple truth. My only message to everyone; be, pray, meditate, and enjoy all of life's gifts. Life is not waiting for us somewhere in the distance nor is it in the past or future: it is here and now, it is moving and dancing within us. Remain open, available, and grateful for every gain or loss that existence offers and never take anything for granted. We are not here to achieve life. We are life. Life cannot be achieved: it is to be realized and lived consciously and significantly.

I am grateful to my parents Mile and Zora without whom I would have not realize what I have realized. I am holding them deeply in my being and I thank them for all of their efforts. My mother was a model of faith, of prayer and of hope for me. She taught me to pray and worship God as the only existing source of freedom and salvation since without Him life has no meaning. My father taught me the importance of integrity as a root of my essence, my honour and my morality. To respect everyone regardless of people's believes, faith, religion or skin colour. He said that human integrity is the most valuable passport in life, and that an honest man does not need to knock at the door because for him every door is wide open.

My great thanks and appreciation to Mooji: the enlightened spiritual Master who helped me see and breakthrough my final delusion. His profound wisdom, compassion, and love for humanity serve as a universal voice of consciousness, truth, and freedom.

Also my high respect and recognition to many other enlightened beings in the world who have given and still give of themselves to the existence for the sake of God's everlasting love and light.

And above all, my profound devotion, honor, and reverence to Jesus Christ and His most Holy Spirit since He was, is, and shall be my dearest refuge and Savior.

Any gain from this book is intended for orphans irrelevant of geographical location.

May there be peace, love, and harmony among all the beings of this Earthly world.

Editing by

Anwesha Roy,

Francois & Noa Gilbert